FROM
EGO TO
Essence

Integrating Spiritual
Living into Everyday Life

ROBIN MASTERS

BALBOA.
PRESS

A DIVISION OF HAY HOUSE

Interior Graphics/Art Credit: Jon James Quinn III

Balboa Press books may be ordered through booksellers or by contacting:

Balboa Press
A Division of Hay House
1663 Liberty Drive
Bloomington, IN 47403
www.balboapress.com
1 (877) 407-4847

Print information available on the last page.

ISBN: 978-1-5043-7333-3 (sc)
ISBN: 978-1-5043-7353-1 (e)

Balboa Press rev. date: 01/18/2017

ACKNOWLEDGEMENTS

I would like to acknowledge and thank my son and photographer, Jon, for the time and effort he placed in producing such beautiful photographs for this book. His work completes the words.

To my daughter, Kaitlin, I would also like to express my thanks, for always listening and being so supportive in her confidence in my ability to write this book.

I would also like to thank my husband, who, without his support, this book may never have been finished. Thank you for your help and for always being there.

For my Mom and Dad...

CONTENTS

Section One

EGO VERSUS ESSENCE

WHY MOVE FROM EGO TO ESSENCE?

It seems like a great effort. What's to gain? Why not just remain living life through ego?

Because living life through ego will never bring happiness, that's why. You will never be at peace. Living life through ego is a constant "wanting" and as soon as one wanting is met, the next wanting comes along. Rarely, if ever, does ego let you sit with and feel the gratitude and happiness you thought you would obtain when you received what your ego told you that you so desperately desired.

Living in ego will never bring you peace, joy or true happiness. The ego is insatiable; as soon as it gets what it desires, instead of taking the time to treat what you received with appreciation and gratitude it wants something newer and better. It always wants more and more and hopefully, someday, we eventually come to the realization that we will never be happy or at peace. We become disillusioned and it is at that moment we finally start to see that there is another way of living.

Living life through Essence opens up worlds of opportunities as you become in tune with the signs and synchronicities which are always out there to guide your life, but went by unnoticed and ignored, lost in the drama of everyday living.

So in order to live through essence its most important to define what essence is and what it is not, and how exactly the ego controls us. It is essential to figure out how to move through and quiet the thoughts of the mind. The more you are able to live life through Essence, the more you are able to integrate spirituality into your life.

THE MASQUE OF EGO

So what exactly is the ego and what purpose does it serve?

To put it simply, we have been brought up to believe that our thoughts create our personality and our ego. We have been brought up to believe that this defines who we are. Many fear that without these thoughts, without the ego and personality, we would not exist. At least, this is what the ego tries to convince us of. But the ego is nothing more than a masque, a façade built over the years to protect that child inside us. It hides our true self from others, and often times from ourselves. However, the ego defining who we are could not be further from the truth. The truth of the matter is that we are not our thoughts, we are not our ego. We are something much, much deeper than that. When we finally get to the bottom of it all, to that last and final layer – we finally have the freedom to feel who we really are. We have the freedom to feel our Essence, to feel the very heart of our soul.

"Thinking", when used correctly, can be an amazing tool for solving problems in personal life as well as problems in the world. It is how we learn, how new creations are invented. But thinking becomes a malady when it stops being used to solve functional issues and begins being used to feed the ego and its drama of everyday living. When thinking becomes so obsessive that it can't be stopped is when it becomes the problem. Many psychological illness, as well as physical ones, can be attributed to the overactive ego thoughts and the stress it places on the body and mind.

There are many out there who refuse to accept that their thoughts and their ego are not the real them for varying reasons. Some are simply unaware and go through their lives just accepting the falsehood of ego. Oftentimes, these people have been brought up not to question things and just accept the values that have been passed down from their parents. But many times the refusal to admit that the ego is nothing more than a protective shell between Essence and society is based on fear; the fear of rejection, the fear of being different and ridiculed, the fear of being ostracized. Just a simple basic fear of vulnerability. The ego makes them feel safe and secure and offers a false promise of protection from all this and the emotional pain it may cause.

Ego seems to have a life of its own and it will work consistently and convincingly to make you believe it is who you are. It's difficult to remember at times that the ego is just a masque and not actually "you". But it's important to understand that ego is nothing more than a collection of thoughts and emotions based on preconceived notions. Ego is nothing more than a façade presented to the world in order to hide your fears and insecurities.

Ego thinks its death is the same as physical death and it will work tirelessly to have you believe it. This is why it creates endless drama; to keep itself alive. Drama is an addiction in society, as evidenced by the endless stream of negative movies and news that people thrive on watching. Many people feel as though they are not really "living", or that their lives are boring without the drama.

There is another way to live, a much, much better more fulfilling way to live and that is a life through Essence.

DEFINING ESSENCE

How do you define something that cannot be fully expressed in words?

Within each and every one of us there resides a self of pure love and acceptance, a self that is eternal and free from attachments. A self that is full of knowledge and that sees the big picture of life, not just its own selfish and personal little world. That self is your Essence and it is the core of who you are.

Everyone has this Essence, this Higher Self. Everyone has this observer who is watching the drama of the ego's personality unfolding in the world. Your Higher Self goes by many different names in varying cultures such as Essence, the Soul, Spirit, your Higher Self, but I prefer the term "Essence" because it is not attached to any particular school of thought. It matters not which expression you choose just don't get caught up in words and use which ever phrase feels the most comfortable for you. Waking up to Essence has been described as such things as enlightenment, awakening, DNA activation, living in the fifth dimension, but it all boils down to the same thing; becoming in contact with your core self.

Living through Essence is a place where you live life understanding there is a bigger picture. Signs and synchronicities are a continual part of your life. It is the connection through the soul to all that is. Only when you experience Essence do you come to understand that words are not capable of describing this state of being. It must be experienced to be understood.

Essence is a surrender to living in the presence. It is not a "giving up" but an acceptance of what is. It is a realization that the drama of everyday life truly means nothing. Many are afraid that by giving into this acceptance they are surrendering their "free will", but free will is not necessarily the choices we make, but how we choose to respond to situations as they are presented to us. You can respond through Essence and live life through peace or you can respond through ego and live life through endless drama. The choice is yours.

EGO VERSUS ESSENCE

When trying to discern between the voice of ego and the voice of Essence, there are very distinct characteristics that belong to each one.

Essence never judges, justifies or makes excuses. Essence will never try to talk you into or out of something.

Essence will never express negativity. Any negative thoughts or emotions belong to ego.

Generally speaking, thoughts that begin with "I" are ego based. "I want", I need", "I feel", all of these expressions indicate ego is behind the thought. Even such a thought as, "I want to help" is ego based. Ego is looking for the satisfaction of saying, "Look what I did, aren't I great!" When your help is warranted and needed it will arise naturally and spontaneously through Essence and it will fill you with a sense of peace that ego is unable to give.

Ego has no patience. It wants it and it wants it NOW! If you really listen from an outside perspective often time's ego sounds like a five year old child throwing a tantrum.

Ego hates the unknown, it hates change, whereas Essence embraces all experience.

The voice of Essence knows, the voice of ego reasons. If you're trying to reason, justify and make excuses; it's Ego talking. Ego is driven by a selfishness, a perspective with one view. Essence sees the bigger picture. It is never judgmental and it never negotiates. If you find yourself reasoning over something, it's ego talking. As we said, Essence **knows** things. It never "decides" something. It shows up as a thought with decisiveness and without question. Any nagging or cajoling, any should or shouldn't, comes from the ego. Essence would never use these words and its voice never ends with a question mark.

Essence receives openly and graciously; ego questions and is never grateful or satisfied.

There is a spontaneity to Essence. Thoughts arrive seemingly out of nowhere, out of the blue and usually it has nothing to do with what you're focusing on at that moment. It happens when the ego is quiet and the mind is occupied with the present moment. It always comes across as a statement and it comes across as a "knowing". Thoughts that come from Essence have a peaceful underlying feeling to them, no matter what the circumstance. You can also connect to Essence through meditation or when you're completely absorbed in something. This could be a hobby you love or perhaps some type of physical activity. Thoughts from Essence always come across as a "knowing" and always feel right and peaceful.

THE DISSOLUTION OF EGO

Ego, by no means goes quickly or quietly. Ego does not give up easily. Sometimes during this process you almost feel as though you're being split in two with ego wanting to go one way and Essence the other. You almost feel as though you're going a little crazy but realizing this is perfectly normal and that everyone goes through it helps to ease the process. Just remember you are not alone in your journey.

Everyday opportunities will present themselves and you will have to make a choice between responding through ego or responding from Essence. Sometimes you will choose ego, and sometimes you will choose Essence. Do not judge or beat yourself up over those times you may choose ego. It is all a learning experience; just observe and accept and maybe the next time the situation presents itself you will respond from Essence.

Don't fight with the ego, the key is truly acceptance. Your ego can be attributed to a small child throwing a tantrum when it doesn't get its way. You don't argue with the child, a time out is usually justified and this is generally what needs to be done with ego. Let it cry itself out while you do little more than observe.

Your ego will never disappear one hundred percent of the time. However, as you learn to be in Essence more and more of the time your ego will start to take a back seat to Essence. Gradually the ego voice will fade until it is nothing more than a whisper we observe and accept.

GETTING IN TOUCH WITH ESSENCE

Separating from ego is by no means an easy feat but once you become aware of the ego's existence it begins to lose its powerful grip. One of the keys to separating is to become an observer of your own life. You do this by taking a step back and "watching" as events unfold in your life, rather than reacting. This may sound difficult and even a little odd, but one way to do this is to become almost like a narrator of your own life. This pulls you out of your mind and out of your thoughts of past and future. It brings you instantly to the present and to the awareness that is essential if you are to get beyond ego and live life through Essence.

Reducing drama is essential. The drama in your life that is created by ego can be reduced if you keep one thing in mind. Your thoughts create your emotions. It may be hard to discern this but try and take notice. It seems to happen simultaneously but if you take a closer look the thought actually comes first and then a split second later the emotion. When you realize this you can stop the thought before the emotion connects. Just remind yourself when an unpleasant emotion arises that you can reduce the hold the emotion has by just the awareness of the situation. When drama is reduced in your life it makes it easier for Essence to shine through.

Simplify. Simplify. Simplify your life. Slow down and cut out those activities that really aren't necessary or that you don't enjoy. When you are constantly running it makes it difficult to hear Essence. Taking time to sit in silence is a great way to connect to Essence. Turn off the phone, turn off the television and just sit. Let your mind wonder, but don't let it settle on any specific thoughts. Let your thoughts just "float". Being still is considered lazy by many, but it is truly an important part of life when trying to connect to Essence.

Coming into your body takes you out of your mind and ego. Exercise and physical activity are a great way to shut up the ego. Anything, hiking, surfing, running; anything that gets the body pumping will work. If you are unable to do anything physical, you can still get into the body by "feeling" each of your body parts. Tell yourself, "I feel my fingers, I feel my toes, I feel my forearms, etc. and actually feel these parts of your body by focusing all your mind on them. This works just as well.

Doing something you love creates a doorway to Essence. Singing, dancing, drawing, golfing – any hobby that you love will do. These things take up your attention and ego is pushed by the wayside. Anytime that happens it quiets the mind, making it easier for a thought from Essence to be heard. Of course, any type of meditation or breathing exercise ignites the same reaction.

Sometimes it may be difficult to hear Essence over all the incessant chatter cluttering your mind. Sometimes ego tries to fool you by imitating Essence. We cannot reach

Essence through the mind, no matter how hard you think about it, analyze it or try to define it – the mind simple cannot grasp the concept. Ego will work endlessly to find a solution to a problem usually a problem it's created itself, but those answers are never found in the mind. Ego can worry, ponder, guess, plan and manipulate any which way it wants and in the end what does it have? Nothing. And if by chance ego does come up with an answer, how often was it right? Usually these thought do nothing more than get in the way of hearing Essence and cause detours from your path.

In order to discover and hear Essence, it is especially important to keep in mind that as stated earlier, you are **not** your thoughts. Be aware, become the observer and try to keep in mind that all the crazy drama is nothing more than a creation of the ego. You are the observer, the watcher, the one who is listening, not the one who is reacting.

A thought coming from Essence feels very different than thoughts of the ego. There are no feelings behind it. No drama or questioning, no confusion. It generally comes across as a statement, almost a command. It can be expressed as an action or a sudden insight. Generally it comes seemingly out of nowhere usually when you are deeply rooted in the present moment. It often feels like that "Ah Ha!" moment when a bulb goes off in your head and suddenly you just "know" the answer. And that's what it feels like, a "knowing". The voice doesn't manipulate or question; it just knows. When you take the time to quiet your ego, even unintentionally, you leave room for Essence to reach through the incessant chatter to be heard.

I saw this for myself when my car was overdue for inspection. I was driving to work, singing with the radio, not even thinking about my car, when out of nowhere I heard this loud, commanding voice in my head say, "Go to motor vehicle". I was right at the turn off that would take me to motor vehicle, or I could continue on going straight to work. In a split second decision I decided to listen to that voice and I turned off to go to motor vehicle, even as part of me told me I was crazy to do so.

My car passed inspection and I headed back to work. About a mile down the road there was a road block lined with police cars and tow trucks. It was a roadside inspection. Had I not stopped to go to inspection, my car would have been towed away. I said a silent thank you and expressed my gratitude. Gradually you learn to trust that voice.

Becoming present in the moment, being here in the now, is essential. Anytime you imagine the future or look back to the past, you are in ego. There are ways to bring yourself present. Becoming the observer is one of them. Doing something you love or something creative, such as singing or drawing, pulls you to the present moment. Sitting in silence, meditation, breathing; these also bring you present. Feelings of gratitude will bring you into the now. Keep all this in mind and you will create a pathway for Essence to be heard.

Every day, every moment, life presents opportunities to make the choice of living through ego or living through Essence. Sometimes you will choose Essence, and sometimes you will choose ego; it's difficult to break old habits. Sometimes it just feels easier to surrender to ego's chatter just because it is what you are used to. Don't beat yourself up for those times you may stumble and choose ego, for it's the ego that does the beating up. Don't judge or criticize; simply observe and learn from the occasion.

Gradually, more and more you will find yourself choosing Essence. Living life through Essence opens up worlds of opportunities as you become more in tune with the signs and synchronicities which Essence presents to guide you on your path.

Section Two

SIGNS AND
SYNCHRONICITIES

SYMBOLS AND SYNCHRONICITY

You cannot talk about communication with Essence without bringing signs and synchronicities into the conversation. Spirit guides also play a major role when it comes to hearing Essence. These are an integral part of the system and connects Essence with purpose. They point the way and reinforce you when you're on the right path. They try and turn you in the other direction when you're heading the wrong way. It's a matter of staying open and receptive and being in tune with what the universe is trying to tell you.

Signs and symbols are developed on a very personal level between Essence and your spirit guides, your angels, the universe, or whatever you choose to call those on the other side that help guide us through life. You may read various books with the meanings of signs and numbers, and this could make for a great starting point but you will find as you begin strengthening communication with the other side, you will come to develop your own meanings for the messages that come into your life. Look for names, numbers, phrases, songs that seem to show up over and over again and you will start to develop a relationship with your guides.

This became evident to me when I start seeing the number four everywhere. At first I just sort of dismissed it, but when I began working at store number 444, I finally began to take notice. The icing on the cake was a receipt I had wrung up for $444.44 at 4:44 in the afternoon at store 444. That got my attention all right. Since I was going through a difficult time in my life I guess they wanted to make sure that I knew they were still there for me. It was quite the comforting feeling.

SYNCHRONISTIC EVENTS

Synchronistic events are very cool to watch unfold. Many write off synchronistic events as nothing more than mere coincidences but truly they go much deeper than that. These are events which occur that initially appear to be unrelated but there is something in each which you might make you to say, "Hey that was a weird coincidence". After which something else happens and something else happens which separately might be considered a coincidence, but put together they are considered synchronistic events. Sometimes these are the very things that lend hope and keep you going at a particularly rough time in your life. Watching these events unfold you may at first think they are unrelated or possibly a mere coincidence but when you look deeper there is usually some kind of causal event that ties them in together. Synchronicities and signs go hand and hand as a means of communication from our spirit guides and the universe.

My first real experience that I can recall dealing with synchronistic events came at a point in my life where things were really rough and I was at a very low point. I felt lost and I was looking for someone to pray to that might listen. In the midst of this I received an email that caught my eye because there was a rose in it and since I collect roses I had hoped that maybe it would be some kind of sign.

It was an email explaining the life of Saint Therese of Lisieux and what caught my eye was that she was also known as Saint Therese of the Little Flowers. It was said that if you were to pray to her she would let you know your prayers were heard by sending a rose in some way or form. This was right up my ally and I felt a little spark of hope – I was sure this was a message from my spirit guides. So I prayed to Saint Therese.

When I didn't see a rose in the next day or so, I kind of forgot about it. Later that week I was on my way to pick up my kids from school. I got there a little early so I decided to take a walk on the beach, which was near their school. It was a cold, dreary day in March and the beach was deserted; there wasn't a soul in sight. As I wondered along watching the waves come in, I couldn't help but feel a little sorry for myself. My situation was bleak – I had lost my job, I was deeply in debt and couldn't even afford the insurance for the car I was driving. I felt as though I had lost my purpose and my way. All my ideas of spirituality and religion had been challenged to the point where I no longer knew what to believe. I felt very much alone.

As I wondered along the beach, I noticed something at the water's edge. As I drew closer I suddenly realized what is was and I let out a surprised gasp. There at the edge of the waves lay a perfect long stem red rose. I stared at it in astonishment for a few moments, then slowly bent down to pick it up. It was in perfect condition, untouched by sand or water. I looked around to see if there was anyone nearby but there wasn't a soul in sight. The beach was completely deserted so it didn't seem possible that someone had just happened to drop it there – it had to have been there for a while and yet it was completely untouched by the elements. As I continued to stare in utter disbelief at this sign I had so desperately prayed for a few days ago, I felt a warm, peaceful glow start to settle over me. I found a sense of relief and peace and I knew suddenly that everything was going to be alright. I gave a silent thank you to St. Therese and headed back to my car with a new found sense of hope.

Roses continued to pop up for me in the strangest of places. Two days later, a very much needed check arrived in the mail. The stamp on the envelope, a rose. Four days later I had an interview for a job. While driving there, I passed a billboard which showed a dozen roses upon it. When I arrived at the place where my interview was, I came to discover that the symbol representing the company was a rose. I got the job and everything started falling into place.

While all this was going on, my ego mind worked so fervently to discredit and undermine the new found faith that came over my heart on that day. It would say, "it was a coincidence, your making too much of it, don't be such a fool". But despite ego's attempts, I couldn't help but feel in my heart that the roses were a message and an answer to my request for a sign. To this day I still pray to St. Therese.

SIGNS FROM ANGELS
AND SPIRIT GUIDES

There are so many ways our spirit guides and angels communicate with us; it's just a matter of being in tune with Essence and being open to receiving the information. When we are too caught up with the drama of everyday life it is difficult to hear what they are trying to say. That is why it is so important to take some time each day to just be still. You don't have to sit cross-legged reciting "ohm" or anything like that, though meditation is definitely helpful. Just sit and be still. Turn of the phones and computers and televisions and the thinking and just sit and be present in the moment. If you have difficulty doing this, especially the thinking part, don't try to stop the thinking, let your mind just float. There is a very simple means of becoming present to the now; just sit and notice all that is around you. Name the things you see and hear. This will pull you out of you ego mind or at the very least, it will quiet it down.

When you're lost in thought, worried over some upcoming event, mulling over what may have happened in the past, you miss the here and now – and the here and now is where these signs take place. You will develop a relationship with your guides and begin to understand the "clues" that come your way. Signs and symbols come in so many ways. Numbers, songs, phrases, a stranger on the street – basically anything can have meaning if you stay alert.

You can ask for help or for a sign to be sent. In fact, you should ask and they will respond. I remember after one difficult breakup I kept hearing songs of mine and my ex over and over again. Anywhere I went I would hear our songs – it was actually ridiculous. Finally I said to my guides, "Enough already! If you really want to help play something inspiring and the song "Calling All Angels" popped into my head which begins with the line "I need a sign". So I said to them, "Yeah, play that song", kind of in a daring manner. Five minutes later, I got into my car to go to work, turned on the radio. Much to my astonishment the exact song I requested was playing and the first lines I heard were, "I need a sign". I actually started laughing. "Alright", I said, "I think you made your point."

I remember at one point in my life there was a burning question in my mind that I pretty much begged my guides to answer but I couldn't seem to hear their answer or figure out what they were trying to tell me. It was a question that could mean a life changing decision. Well, there was a little metaphysical shop which had opened up in my town that I had wanted to check out, but every time I passed by it was closed. One day I had to bring a package to the post office, which was right next door and on that day the door to the shop was wide open with a big inviting sign next to it.

I was in the market for some new books and here was the opportunity. As I walked in the scent of incense filled my nostrils and there was soothing meditation music playing; overall a very inviting and comfortable atmosphere. There was an elderly woman at the register and she gave me a warm smile. "Is there anything special I can help you with?" I told her I was interested in looking for the book section and she directed me to the back of the store.

While I tried to find something of interest within the dusty shelves, the woman came back to talk to me. She told me she was offering angel readings for half price. I politely thanked her but declined the offer. I chose two books and proceeded to the checkout counter. As the woman totaled my sale, she pointed to a small jar with folded pieces of paper. She told me to pick one out and it would be a message from my angels. I chose one and laughed when I read out loud; "be spontaneous" it said. So the woman said to me, "Maybe they want you to be spontaneous and have a reading." I laughed again and joked that they all probably said the same thing. I thanked her for her help and left the shop.

As I drove away, I couldn't get this nagging feeling out of my mind that perhaps I should have stayed for a reading. I didn't believe much in psychic readings and I hated to waste money on something as frivolous as a reading since I didn't have much faith in the whole psychic thing, but I couldn't get rid of the nagging feeling. Before I knew it, I found myself turning around and heading back to the shop. "Change your mind?" The woman at the counter smiled when I walked in. "I had a feeling you'd be back." I laughed and said, "Yeah, I think the 'be spontaneous' might have had something to do with it."

She led me to the back of the store where we sat at a small table behind a curtain. Candles and incense were everywhere and there was a deck of cards on the table. Before I was able to even touch the cards or say a word she seemed surprised and said, "Your angels, it's almost rude, they're practically shouting at me. They want you to know..." and she proceeded to answer the question that had been burning in my mind for years. I was stunned! She used the exact same words, the same terminology, answering the question I had wanted an answer to for so long. How could this woman possibly pull this response out of thin air without asking me a word?

I don't remember much else after that. I know I picked a few cards and she predicted of few things that eventually came true but I never forgot that experience and the faith that came with it. As much as I racked my brain trying to come up with a logical explanation, I could come up nothing. I went to go to the shop again the following week and it was gone. Closed up. Just like that. I was so disappointed I couldn't help but feel it as though the shop had stayed there just long enough for me to hear from my guides. I wish I had gotten the woman's name and number, I would love to have spoken to her again.

My angels and guides have a sense of humor as well. I remember back to when online dating was becoming really popular, and I was checking out one of their web sites. I wondered if such a concept as meeting someone on line could actually work. It seemed weird to me going through all the pictures of these strangers, but finally, someone caught my eye. I tried to come up with a clever response of some kind, but became frustrated not really knowing what to say. I got up from my desk, pushed the chair in hard and said to my guides a little sarcastically, "Well, if it was meant to be, he'll find me".

Fast forward a few months, my life is turned upside down when I totaled my car and when I lost my job in the same week. Though I had not had any intention of it I suddenly found myself back in school, a place I never thought I would be. Guess who I met there? Yup, the guy from the web site I was going to respond to. How did that end up? Well, we got married.

SIGNS FROM LOVED ONES

Some of the most fulfilling and exciting signs comes from our loved ones who have passed on. What a feeling of comfort to know they are still there and still very much a part of our lives. These signs may show up in so many different ways and are usually extremely personal. It could be a song, a fragrance, a picture falls over while you are talking about them. The ways are unlimited.

One of my favorite stories is the tale about Pennies from Heaven. I had never heard of this until one night when I was cleaning up at the retail store I worked at when one of the girls found a penny on the floor. She picked it up to check the year and said she received a chill when she saw the date; it was the year her mother had died. She explained to me that pennies are messages from the angels and our loved ones and they usually express a significant date such as a birthday or a passing year. I loved this idea and I wanted a penny of my own. I prayed to my dad, who had passed when I was younger, asking him if he could possibly please send me a penny.

A few days later I was working on a merchandising change which involved taking one set of clothes off the wall and replacing them with a newer set. I needed to rearrange the fixtures for the group so I was on a ladder, about six feet up, moving the shelves higher. The store was designed with slat walls where the fixtures just slid right in to them, which made the job significantly easier. As I perched on top of the ladder, something shiny caught my eye. Wedged into one of the slats was a penny. It was bent and stuck so tight that I needed a screwdriver to pry it out. I held my breath as I looked at the date. 1993. The year my dad passed away. My heart was pounding and tears came to my eyes as I kept staring at the date in disbelief. I could hardly believe that in one of the most unlikely places to find a penny I had found one with the most significant date. How could I possibly call it a coincidence? What are the odds of such a thing happening? I knew in my heart that my dad had heard me and had sent me one of the best present I had ever received in my life. A sense of peace washed over me and I thanked my dad from the bottom of my heart for such an amazing answer to my prayer.

To top things off, later that day the cutest little boy came into the store. I noticed him because he looked very much like my brothers and my son at that age. He was very chatty with me and I listened to him talk until his mother called out to him, "Time to go, Frank." I was stunned. Frank was my father's name. It's not very common anymore, and in fact, I never actually met a child name Frank before. Another sign? This further cemented my belief that my dad was nearby watching.

My dad helped me out quite a few times and continues to do so. One of my favorite times was when I had gone back to college. Even though I was a paralegal major, it was still required that I take a gym class. Having no athletic ability whatsoever, I tried to find the least offensive class and that happened to be golf. I thought I might have a shot at it because when I was a child, my dad would take my sister and I almost every weekend to play miniature golf. My dad loved to play golf and sometimes we would even watch him practice. Unfortunately, practice putting from my childhood did nothing to help my game. I was down to the wire, my final chance on my final exam, and it was a make or break situation. You had to earn points and depending upon where the ball landed determined the number of points. A basket tied to a pole in the center was an automatic A. I missed shot after shot – I could never get the ball airborne and could do nothing more than chip to the left. On my last shot I said to myself, "Dad, I need help here. Please, please, please help!" I lined up and took my shot – it chipped on the ground to the left as always. My heart started sinking but then, the ball hit rock, bounced up in the air and landed right in the basket! My coach just looked at me and said, "Well, sometimes it's better to be lucky than good". But I knew it wasn't luck; it was my dad and I thanked him profusely over and over again.

My dad sent my son a sign as well. My son was four days shy of two when my dad passed. Instead of a birthday party there was a wake for my dad. My dad was my son's favorite person in the world, he absolutely adored him and he was adored right back. They were great buddies. How do you explain to a two year old why someone just disappears from their life? Well, it was maybe a year and a half later and my son and I were looking at pictures when he pointed to one and said, "That's your dad, isn't it?" I told him it was and he replied "I'm mad at him. He went away and never said goodbye!" Can I tell you how my heart broke at that moment? I fought back tears trying to explain to him something I couldn't understand myself.

The next morning when my son got up he asked, "Did you see your dad when he was here last night? "I was a little startled by the question and asked him if he spoke to him when he saw him, to which he replied "yes", and then he told me he wasn't mad at my dad anymore because he came to say goodbye. I thought he probably just had a dream since we were looking at pictures the day before, but then something interesting happened later that day. I was telling the story to my mother in law when my daughter, who was not quite a year, crawled over to the table, pulled herself up, grabbed the picture of my dad and presented us with the picture. My mother in law at the time and I were both stunned. My daughter had never even met my dad and she wasn't looking at pictures with us the day before; she was napping at the time. Coincidence? I doubt it since the two shared a room and I assume my dad visited with my daughter as well.

I learned for myself that dreams are not always just dreams. I had a dream about a loved one in which he came to me to say goodbye. In the dream his body was fading away and he was saying goodbye for now but he said it would not be forever. In the dream I was so upset because as I said to him, "but I won't be able to see you or touch you anymore". But while I was so upset on the surface, under it all was a deep rooted feeling of peace because I knew without a doubt that we would be together again someday, just not in the same way. The dream felt so real and we hadn't spoken for a bit so I become concerned and tried to find out about him, but not being computer savvy I was unable to locate anything about him on the internet. About ten months later I came to find out that he had passed away in September, the same month that I had the dream. I just couldn't believe it. I was and still am so grateful to him for coming to say goodbye to me and to assure me we would see each other again.

Another sign I received from him took my breath away as well. I was speaking with his mother and the subject how much he loved dragons came up. His mom was saying how it was probably because she always sang him that song, "Puff the Magic Dragon" when he was a baby. Now that's not exactly a song you hear too much about lately. Well that night, I signed onto my music account to discover that under the "my recommendations" section, the first song listed was "Puff the Magic Dragon". I thought this was so cool and I thanked him again for yet another great sign. And when I was telling this story to someone at work she pointed and said "there's a penny by your foot". I picked it up and sure enough it was 2014, the year he passed. A few days later I found a penny from 1965, the year he was born.

My penny collection has grown. Please don't think that I spend my days checking dates of thousands of pennies; generally they find me. I found one from the year my grandmother passed and I found it on Mother's Day. I found a 1944 penny which as I've explained is my number sign from my angels, as well as several more from my dad including one from 1930, the year he was born.

My point here is that with being open and paying attention to the present moment, with time you will develop your own personal system of symbols with your spirit guides. Living life through Essence makes it so much easier to see the signs and synchronicities which enables you to become a part of the flow of life – which is where you want to be.

Section Three

THE FLOW

WHAT IS THE FLOW?

There is a lot of talk within the spiritual community about being "in the flow', but what exactly does this mean?

Living in the flow is a way of living life connected to Essence. It can be described as a state of "being", not as much as a state of "doing". It is a way of living in which you are in tune with and trust your higher self and the signs from the universe. It is a state of acceptance. When you are in the flow you are open and accepting of what life has to offer, and you accept it graciously. You don't add judgements, you don't question and you don't let the ego put a spin on it. It is a matter of trust. When you are in the flow you can't imagine living life any other way. Being in the flow and living life through Essence go hand in hand. When you are out of the flow you are disconnected from Essence and nothing seems to go right. When you try to fight your way back there's a catch 22 because you cannot fight your way back or struggle in any way. This just pushes you further and further in the opposite direction. This comes from the fact that being in the flow is not about "doing" it is about "being". Only through acceptance and going with the flow can you find your way back; it cannot be forced or controlled.

While the flow may be about acceptance and being,

it does not necessarily mean a state of inaction or about being stagnant. Every day you need to do what you can on your part with the resources presented to you. Every day think about what you can do on **that** day with what's available to you, and not be overwhelmed with thinking about everything you may need to do in the future. When you do this, things just fall into place. However, nothing will fall into place if you sit home and ignore the directions and signs your spirit guides may offer to you.

WORKING WITH THE FLOW

Let's say, for instance, you're interested in acting, but you don't know where or how to begin. You're reading the paper that night when you come across an advertisement for a local audition for a play in a small town. On the one hand, your ego feels it is beneath you because it's such a small forum to perform at and ego contemplates not even attending the audition, thinking nothing could possibly come from it. But on the other hand, absolutely nothing will be accomplished if you sit home doing nothing. Not trying, you're guaranteed to have no results whatsoever. So what the heck, you decide to give it a shot and land yourself a nice role. Let's say then, for instance, one night an important director happens to be in the audience. It turns out that maybe his niece or nephew or someone else he knows is in the play. You impress him so much that he contacts you regarding a play he's directing on Broadway. You end up with a small role that eventually turns out to be your big break and the next thing you know you are starring in a Broadway show. See how one thing can lead to another, even if it's the tiniest of moves. You always need to do whatever it is you can with the situations presented to you, no matter how big or small. Had you ignored that first small play, you would still be home, sitting on the couch. Instead, now you're a star.

That is exactly what I did when I discussed going back to college earlier. While the task itself seemed greatly overwhelming, when I broke it down to what I had to do on that day which needed taking care of, it wasn't so scary. Before I knew it, everything had fallen into place and I was at school. Don't be intimidated by seemingly large tasks. Break them down one step at a time and the flow will show you which way to go and what to do next. When you do this things do seem not so overwhelming.

Unfortunately, so much of what we are taught growing up only succeeds in increasing the amount of pressure and stress which takes you further and further away from the flow and Essence. It is the accepted norm in our society that our minds are occupied with thoughts from the past or worries and plans for the future. These things pull you out of the present moment, take you away from Essence, and spin you in the opposite direction from the flow. Most people go through life never questioning their thoughts or knowing there's another way to live. The ego is in control and as stated, many believe this is who they are. Ego pulls us out of the flow by its constant need of being in control, making it almost impossible to hear Essence and the signs it tries to send our way.

TRUSTING THE FLOW

A big part of being in the flow requires trust since you can't see what's coming next. Unfortunately, not knowing things causes great anxiety for the ego. Therefore it will go to great lengths creating stories about what is and what is not going to be. Whether these stores are true or not doesn't really matter. The ego is very convincing. Ego is all about wants and needs, however, the moment it gets what it so desperately needed it's on to the next wanting, as was already stated. It's never happy or satisfied. Ego pulls you out of the flow with its stories and its need to be in control. Believing these stories may lead you away from the direction you were meant to be going.

As we learn to grow and live in the flow of life's everyday moments, you become better prepared for the bigger challenges that may present themselves. When you feel yourself starting to struggle against what's happening in your life you must "accept" your resistance. This may sound strange and impossible, to "accept resistance", but you do this by becoming the observer of your life, just as you do when you are trying to hear Essence through the chatter of the mind. Stop, watch and accept – it's the only way through.

Sometimes things happen in life and in the flow which seem to make no sense and we begin to question what is going on. It's essential to keep the Big Picture in mind. It's important to remember that life is all inclusive with an entire world being involved. The big picture includes all that is going on and everything may not always be about you, but about someone else's life you may touch. You may not always realize the impact your life may have on someone else. You may not always know why something happened, which can be extremely frustrating, but be assured there is a reason for everything, even if that reason doesn't present itself right at that moment. Learn to accept and let life flow instead of struggling against it. It's hard for ego not to question what goes on, but life goes much more smoothly and peacefully when you learn to accept and go with the flow.

Let's say for instance, you were reading a book about enlightenment and let's say you lost this book somewhere. You could lament about how unfair life is and huff and puff with annoyance that you have to go buy a new book. There doesn't seem to be much of a point in this instance, right? However, let's say there is a person somewhere who is desperately praying for help and guidance, praying for a sign. They get on that same bus to go home and they take the only seat left, and there, on this empty seat, there is the book you lost. That person picks it up and suddenly, there's the sign they were looking for. The book has the exact words that they needed to hear to guide their life back on the path. That's the "big picture" – it's not always about us.

Sometimes it may take a while for the flow to make it clear where you're heading. When you've been "waiting" or in limbo for what may seem like an endless amount of time, it's only natural to begin to lose patience and to start questioning ourselves and the existence of the flow. This creates turbulence which then causes resistance as negative emotions begin to build. This turbulence, this resistance creates a negative force which works against the flow. We doubt the flow, and sometimes, even doubt our sanity. We feel forgotten and angry, maybe even a little foolish for believing that the flow would guide us. What we cannot see are the things going on behind the scene working on getting us to where we need to be. What we cannot see is that we are being guided. Sometimes it's just a matter of needing some space because there are times for action and times for inaction and reflection. Again, acceptance is the key to avoid negative emotions from interfering with the natural flow. We need to accept what is happening by being in the present moment without labeling or judging.

THE FLOW AND SYNCHRONICITY

It's important to remember that the flow and synchronicity go hand in hand. Sometimes, when it seems as though nothing is happening, everything begins to happen at once. I experienced this for myself when I lost my job and my car in the same week. I was unexpectedly laid off, my car was totaled and suddenly I had a lot of free time on my hands. What was odd was that amidst all that was happening, deep down I felt a sense of peace, a calmness I couldn't explain, as though somehow I knew, everything was going to be alright. I had felt for quite a while that I needed a change in my life and I was sure this was a sign to move onto something else, but I had no idea what that change might be. A week went by, then two weeks. When a month had passed and I did not seem to be getting any signs, I began to feel a little panicky. My confidence in the flow began to dwindle and I started to feel a little angry not to mention, a little foolish about my beliefs.

Then one day I received in the mail a flyer for an open

house at the local college. I just dismissed it, it never crossed my mind to go back to school. Suddenly I began to see ads for the college everywhere I turned. On the TV, on the radio, in the newspaper. There was even a large poster staring me in the face as I waited in line at the unemployment office. Everywhere I went there seemed to be ads pointing toward the college. Were these my signs? I decided to check it out.

I went to the open house advertised in the flyer and things began to escalate from there. Although it seemed like a daunting task, I made the decision to go back to school and with that decision everything just started to fall into place. Everything I needed just kind of fell into place. School was covered by financial aid so money wasn't an issue. I received a phone call about a part time job which had become available so I would have some kind of income to help me get through. Shortly thereafter a phone call came through about a car for sale right in my budget and I had transportation to replace the car I lost, enabling me to get to class. Suddenly everything was covered. Oh, and not to mention the fact that I was to meet my future husband at school. It all fell neatly and easily into place. I was in the flow, grateful to be there and sorry that I had ever doubted it.

LOSING THE NEED TO PLAN

One of the quickest ways to become a part of the flow is by letting go of the need to plan. Society not only likes planning, but also encourages it; ego likes and needs it that way, too. You are supposed to have some sort of "life plan" to be considered a productive part of society and those who don't plan, such as the "drifters", are considered to be lazy and unmotivated. Your ego is more concerned with how you present yourself to others than what is actually good for you. Planning isn't necessarily a bad thing, but when you become so caught up on how things are "supposed" to be that you cannot hear Essence or see the signs, the planning may begin to interfere with the direction of the flow.

Then there are those who take it to the opposite extreme. I've read books that have stated that in order to be in the flow you need to up and quit your job and immediately just start doing what you love. Let's face it; that's really not feasible, especially if you have a mortgage or rent, or have children. Quitting your job if you're not ready or running off on a retreat will work against you and things will not go smoothly if the timing is off or it's just not meant to be. Stumbling blocks will pop up if you're heading in the wrong direction, things like flat tires, traffic, illness, unexpected events; there are many ways that the universe will tell you that you're going the wrong way. This is why you need to work to integrate Essence into your everyday life. If you just relax and go with it, you will suddenly find out that the flow has found you. If you were meant to give up your job or go off on a retreat, or any number of things, the signs will show you the way.

In every moment life changes and moves forward whether you want it to or not. You can struggle and swim against it or grab an oar and go with it; it's your call. The one thing you cannot do is stop it. Your experience is defined not by which way the flow is taking you, but by the way you respond and react to the situation as the flow presents it. That's all you can control – whether you choose to respond from ego or Essence.

THE LAW OF ATTRACTION
AND GRATITUDE

UNDERSTANDING THE LAW

So many people seem to look at the Law of Attraction as a means to gaining all the "material" things the ego feels it needs in life. People tend to look for something specific and when it doesn't' arrive in just the way they wanted it, they feel the law just doesn't work. They become disappointed and disillusioned with the entire concept of the Law of Attraction. Negativity then sets in, creating further resistance for any type of positivity or achievements.

The Law of Attraction is an Essence thing, not an ego thing, so that's not exactly how it works. Let's say for instance you really need a car, and what your ego really wants is a Mercedes Benz. Your ego feels that this is a status symbol that will elevate other people's opinions you. However, Essence has no need for flashy status symbols so the universe does not always deliver what is requested by the ego mind. What you really need is transportation to work. The universe will send answers, but possibly not in the form of what you asked for. Perhaps a bus stop is installed right in front of your house. Or maybe a second hand car becomes available. Not exactly what you wanted, but it does fulfill the need, which was a way to get to work. The universe does not always deliver what the ego mind asks for, but it will move mountains to help fulfill Essence's life purpose.

That being said, since like attracts like, if you can keep your thoughts positive and uplifted, that is what you will attract into your life. Negative thoughts will bring negative situations. There is nothing wrong with requesting something, but you need to be open to the ways in which the universe may present what you may need. Besides, even if the ego does get what it so desperately wants, there's no chance to bask in the glory of attainment. As quickly as you receive what you wanted the ego begins to criticize, judge or even reject it. It finds fault and comes up with reasons why it is no longer good enough, why it no longer suits us and it begins yet another futile search for satisfaction. It an endless cycle that is doomed to fail if you let ego run the show. Getting a handle on our thoughts and not letting ego call the shots, you will find your thoughts will be much more open and positive.

Ask for what you want, but be open to how it arrives. Many times people tend to pass over the little opportunities because they have a "big grand scheme" in mind. Sometimes, though, these little opportunities are the very stepping stones which may lead to where you want to go or to achieve what it is you want to achieve.

THOUGHT VS. EMOTION

Which comes first, the thought or the emotion? It may feel as though they arrive simultaneously, but this is not the case. Your thoughts come first even if it's just a fraction of a second prior to the emotion. Observe this and you will see. Once you realize that your thoughts create your feelings and emotions, then if you don't want to feel a certain way all you need to do is change the thought. Sounds simple enough, right? But it's not that simple in reality. Your need to dismiss the thought before any emotion attaches to it, but sometimes you may not even be consciously aware of the thought until the feelings begin to arise. Knowing this, if you can train your thoughts to be positive, you will attract positive things to come your way.

Start this process by just becoming aware. Catch yourself as soon as you start to feel an emotion arise then change the thought. Bring yourself back into the present moment by asking yourself, "Does this thought really suit me? Is this where I want to be? Is this what I want to feel? If your answer in no then stop the thoughts right in their tracks. If you can't seem to stop it, try starting another line of thinking, which could work as a distraction. Move your attention to something else and don't let your mind linger in a place it where it really shouldn't be.

Observing your thoughts to redirect them in a different direction sounds simple, but it is not easy. It takes work; work and consciously being aware of what's going on in your mind and you must have the willingness to let go of unwanted thoughts. Over time, this will become a way of life. Just remember, you, not your ego, has the power to redirect your thoughts.

Don't get discouraged. It can really take a while before your new "positive" way of thinking permanently implants itself in your mind. Trying to pretend or talk positive when you're in a negative place, just doesn't really work. Again, just accept the negativity, observe it, and it will fade away. If anything trying to fight your negative thoughts will just fuel the situation because resistance never works. The challenge of changing your thoughts becomes a choice which presents itself on a daily basis. Over and over you will be asked to choose. Respond from ego or respond from Essence. Sometimes you will choose Essence and sometimes you won't. The key is to not beat yourself up for those times that your response comes from ego. Don't judge, don't make yourself wrong, merely observe the decision and the consequences. Now that you have awareness, now that you are conscious of the fact that there is another way, you become closer to Essence and the hold from ego is weakened.

OWNING YOUR JUDGMENTS

What is meant by the term "owning your judgments"?

The people we cultivate relationships with and the challenges they present can be one of your greatest teachers. They also tend to be the people we judge the harshest, except for maybe ourselves. When we judge the things we don't like or approve of the negative force behind it hinders our ability to be positive or grateful. All judgements come from ego; Essence never judges or criticizes.

When we "own our judgements" we realize that what we are judging is not about the other person or situation, but about ourselves. Many times the things we judge the harshest in others are the things we see in ourselves, but don't like, or can't admit. We try to ignore them in ourselves. Once we realize this, however, those things we don't like come up to the surface where we can deal with them.

Have compassion, not judgement for others, as well as

for yourself. You never know how you may respond if it were you in the same situation someone else may be in. I know I, myself, have judged others only to find myself in the same situation, reacting just as they had. Put yourself in someone else's shoes, as the saying goes. Try to be understanding and always try to have a sense of compassion for any given person or situation. Remember, responding from Essence will bring you these feelings.

Judgement is an ego thing that sends out negativity which, in turn, may come back to haunt you. Only by becoming aware of our judgements can we lessen the impact and learn to remain in a positive frame of mind. However, don't judge yourself when you find yourself judging others. Just remain aware and become the observer in your life. Judging a judgement is just as bad as the original judgement and sends just as much negativity. Be the unbiased observer and just watch and strive to respond better next time; try to respond from Essence and try to respond with compassion.

THE IMPORTANCE OF GRATITUDE

Gratitude is defined as a "feeling of being thankful", but what exactly does this really mean? I had always considered myself a grateful person, always saying thank you when the situation warranted it, but then when I sat down and really thought about it, I realized feeling grateful means so much very more than that. Being grateful goes much deeper than just a thank you to someone. Being grateful is a very big part of the Law of Attraction; the two go hand in hand.

When you are truly grateful for something, this sends out positive vibes to the universe, which in turn sends positive vibes back your way. This is a great way to reinforce the Law of Attraction.

The reality is, every complaint, every negative thought, pretty much every time you refuse to accept what is happening in the moment, is a display of lack of gratitude. Let's say, for instance, you stub your toe. The instant response tends to be, "Damn, that hurt! Why do bad things always seem to happen to me"! This sends out negativity that you really don't want coming back your way. Now I know stubbing a toe is not a good thing but look at it from a different perspective. Instead of complaining, think of it this way; be grateful you didn't trip, fall and get hurt worse. Or be grateful you didn't break the toe. This can apply to most situations. Another example; you are heading to work, running late for a meeting, when suddenly, someone cuts you off and proceeds to drive under the speed limit. When something like that happens it is very easy to succumb to anger or even a feeling of road rage. As you proceed, up ahead you come upon a four car accident that had just happened. If the guy in front of you hadn't cut you off, you may have become part of that accident. Instead of being angry at the guy, say a prayer of thanks that you were not a part of that accident. Or there may have been a cop up ahead, just waiting to pull over someone speeding to get to work on time. Either way, be grateful to the guy that slowed you down. You never know what's ahead of you.

You really don't ever know what lays in store for you up ahead in life. Keep the big picture in mind when situations such as the ones above happens to you. See life through Essence, keeping in mind that though you may not understand what is happening or why, everything is a part of a bigger plan. You can relate gratitude to any situation. There will always be something to feel grateful for. Sometimes you might not know in the moment why something happens; sometimes you may never know. This is a major frustration for ego, but Essence will always feel grateful in any situation.

APPLYING GRATITUDE TO LIFE

Realize and take notice of your behavior, once again, becoming the observer of your life. Once awareness is present change in your behavior can occur, and you will see things more and more through the eyes of Essence. Gratitude is essential in turning your life around and learning to see things on a daily basis through Essence. Wake up each morning and start your day with a prayer of gratitude.

Keeping a gratitude journal is an excellent way to reinforce the positive vibes the Law of Attraction needs to work, as well as keeping you seeing things through the eyes of Essence. Actually write down on a daily basis the things you feel grateful for. You will realize that you can always find something that occurred during your day that you can feel grateful for. Even the simplest of things; work went well, someone brought you a cup of coffee, the kids were on their best behavior. No matter what, no matter how big or small, there will always be something to write about. Keeping a gratitude journal will remind you to stay in that grateful frame of mind and send positive thoughts and emotions out into the universe, which in turn will send more positive things your way; more things to be grateful for.

Carry around some kind of reminder with you to reinforce the feeling of gratitude. It could be a bracelet, or a ring or a necklace. It could be a special stone or some kind of memento. Just something you can keep with you to remind yourself when things may start to get a little tough. This item can remind you that there is always something to be grateful for.

End each day with thinking about the things that occurred during the day that you are grateful for. After a time, this will become a habit which will turn your life around for the better. It is great reinforcement for the Law of Attraction, as well as a great way to help go through life living through Essence.

Section Five

EVERYDAY LIFE

ESSENCE IN SOCIETY

If you're having a little difficulty integrating Essence into daily life and society, you are not alone. In a society where thinking is a malady, violence is romanticized and materialism is a raging epidemic, it can be difficult to set aside the time and place to make room for Essence to shine through. It can be difficult to make the room and find the time to just sit and feel grateful. That is why it is essential to make Essence a way of life and not just something you think about once in a while.

It can be discouraging when those around you are all responding to situations from ego and you're trying to respond through Essence. It's not easy to integrate the spiritual world with society as it is today. People struggling to hide their insecurities has become the norm in society. To allow yourself to be vulnerable and not take everything personally can be a little frightening. However, once you are in the flow and starting to live through Essence, you're not going to want to go back to your old ways. Remember awareness and observation are the key.

The more you live through Essence and join the flow, the more you live life with gratitude in your heart, the more situations will arise that allow you to remain in the flow. You may start to find your circle of friends is changing as more people of a like mind are drawn to you. The universe will begin sending you people and situations to help guide you through the flow and to help reinforce you living through Essence.

Learn to forgive those around you that haven't yet learned the difference between living life through Essence versus ego. Holding onto anger will impair your ability to let Essence shine through and hinder your feelings of gratitude. Remember don't judge others for their beliefs – remain the observer and accept what goes on around you. Respond from Essence when you are able and don't judge yourself for those times you respond from ego. There is always another choice next time.

ESSENCE AT WORK

Don't forget your path just because you're at work. If you aren't happy with your job, don't try to convince yourself you love it; it won't work and you will just be repressing feelings. Accept the fact that you are not happy, but realize the things about your job that make you feel grateful. You could be grateful that you have a job, grateful that you have the money to pay your bills or take care of your children. As stated earlier, there is always something to be grateful for.

One of the things I realized was that while my job may not be important in the traditional sense, it wasn't exactly brain surgery or anything like that, but it brought me in contact with many people throughout the day. This meant that my life touched many other lives, and I had the power to determine how each encounter could possibly go. With every person I dealt with during the day, and anyone who has ever worked in retail can tell you, at times, this could be no easy task, I had the chance to learn something. Each encounter gave me the opportunity to decide if I would approach this person through ego or Essence. How I treated that person could actually change the course of their day. If someone came into the store in a bad mood and chose to take it out on me (which again, anyone who has ever worked in retail can testify to happening frequently) and then I chose to respond from an ego stand point; the situation could get quite ugly very quickly as two egos clashed, with both of us taking everything from a personal stand point. Each of us may then go on through the day, treating others with the same negativity, and then that person may turn around and do the same, and so on. That's a lot of negativity stemming from just one incident.

On the other hand, if I could approach the situation through Essence, if I could not take it personally, if I could see the bigger picture and understand it wasn't necessarily about me, the outcome could be totally different. Having no idea what may have put this person in a bad mood in the first place, if I could put aside my ego and respond out of the compassion that is Essence, maybe I could turn that persons day around. Then maybe they would, in turn, go out and do something nice for the next person and that would be the chain for the day; instead of negativity, positivity and good things could come of it. What all this means is that, whether you realize it or not, you hold a lot of power in your hands. Your words and actions actually do have an impact on what goes on in the world.

Of course, doing this is much easier said than done. Remaining in Essence in a world of egos can be quite challenging. I tried to look at it as if I were going to school. I would wake up in the morning, give myself a pep talk, determined to be a good student; ready to master the ego and live my day through Essence. I would be feeling really positive and I would be sure that this would be the day I would handle all situations through Essence. I'd be "pep-talking" myself all the way to work and yet somehow, every day by the end of the day, I would go home feeling like a failure. I could see the person I wanted to be, and there would be moments when Essence would shine through, but then there always seemed to be that one person who would push my buttons and push me over the edge. At those moments I would feel like a hypocrite and a fake for feeling one way in the morning and the total opposite way when I got home at night. I would feel like I had failed my "quiz", so to speak.

While dealing with the public everyday could be a challenge, it was probably the best "schooling" to advance my cause. I just needed to start thinking about things differently. Until I started to accept, though I didn't want to, that work was actually a part of my path, nothing would change. I had to accept that I was in the perfect classroom for what I had to learn, with each interaction being an opportunity to choose to respond from ego or from Essence. It was a part of my journey.

Awareness is key. When you are aware without judging yourself, much can be learned from these situations at work. You just can't be so hard on yourself. If you find yourself slipping into your old ways, which of course will happen, don't beat yourself up about it. Just be aware and forgive yourself and know you can make a different choice next time. The awareness and the knowing is a lesson in of itself. Your path is still there; it's not going anywhere. There's no rush, no time frame, no destination; it's all about the journey. Sometimes we just forget this.

And every now and again, when you are dealing with the public, you get to see "karma" in action. For instance, one day at my retail job, we had a very nasty woman who spoke horribly to everyone in the store. She made her purchase and left the store, only to return twenty minutes later – turned out she had lost her car keys. Had she been a little nicer, maybe something like that would not have happened to her.

THE NEXT GENERATION

"We were raised like that and we all turned out all right." How many times have you heard that expression? Are we all really all right? Dysfunctional might be a better word. Had we been raised to live life through Essence, what a different world it would be.

Working in a children's clothing store has given me a firsthand look at the relationships between small children and their parents. It seems that many moms are more focused on their shopping and their phones, barely acknowledging their children or even giving them a second glance. It always amazed me how often a child would wander out the door, to be retrieved by a sales associate, and the mom didn't even realize their child had left the building. We even had a child left behind because their parent left the store and forget her.

Quality time with children is diminished as parents and care givers are so focused on their phones and computers that there is little acknowledgement given to the children. Not to mention, kids are glued to their electronic devices. The age of technology has created a multitude of babysitters through the internet, video games and DVDs. While having these things could be a definite plus with the knowledge they present at your fingertips, more often than not they are abused.

Today's children are busier than ever, but at what cost? The pressure is intense and it starts at a young age. Most kids start school before they are even two years old. School begins earlier and ends later, homework is much more intense. Any free moment is filled with dance or soccer or baseball, or any other hobby you can think of, including video games. They have no time to just sit and be, which is essential for not only adults, but children as well. Many are burned out before they even finish high school.

Today's children are raised with more exposure to violence than previous generations. The internet, video games, news programs; all can lead to major exposure to violence. Materialism is out an all-time high and yet despite the money and mcmansions, children are seeing that it doesn't bring happiness to their parents.

At younger ages, children are questioning the meaning of life, questioning their purpose in life. Without proper guidance, they may become lost in a questioning despair. If we can teach them at a young age the difference between ego and Essence, teach them about judgement and gratitude, the difference it could make in their lives would be amazing. If children were brought up understanding these basic concepts, then acceptance and Essence would become the norm. Remember, treating children with respect will teach respect. Treating children through Essence will teach them to live through Essence.

Section Six

PRACTICES TO KEEP
YOU IN ESSENCE

IN CLOSING...

Shifting from ego to Essence is an ongoing journey. Challenges will present themselves day in and day out. At every moment, there is a choice to respond from ego or respond through Essence. It is a gradual process. Some days you will choose Essence and other days it will be ego.

There are times when all this can seem so frustrating, especially on those really rough days at work or the kids are misbehaving, or when friends are being unusually dramatic. But you've seen that glimpse, you know it's there, the peace and joy that accompany living life through Essence. You've experienced that warm glow which permeates your being when you respond to situations as such, no matter what drama may have unfolded.

Don't get discouraged if some days you feel as though you take two steps forward three steps back. It happens to everyone and always remember, the best way to get back into essence is through acceptance and gratitude and even if you are unable to feel grateful in that moment – don't fight it or beat yourself up, just accept it and let it be.

The following are practices you can implement on a daily basis. These practices, while not a cure all, will most definitely help you on your path to living life in Essence. While by no means this is easy, life is a journey, not a destination – always remember that!

PRACTICES TO KEEP YOU
CONNECTED TO ESSENCE

Sometimes life circumstances throws you a curve that jolts you right out of Essence right back smack dab back into ego. At these times it is especially important to maintain daily practices which can help keep you connected to Essence. Even if in that moment you don't feel as though these practice are working, keep going and don't get discouraged.

- Start your day with a prayer of gratitude and end your day with a prayer of gratitude
- Practice mindful meditation or present moment awareness. If a structured meditation is truly something you can't sit still for, then sit for ten minutes a day in a quiet place and just notice the things around you. Saying them out loud can keep your mind from wondering. Name things, "I see the clouds, I hear the birds, I smell honeysuckle…" and so on. This pulls you right back into present moment awareness and opens a doorway for Essence to enter.
- It is important to try and always remember that you are not your thoughts, you are the one observing those thoughts. It is not the thought itself that creates the negativity, but the emotion that attaches to it. While this seems to happen simultaneously, there is a gap, however brief, from the time the thought occurs until the emotion takes over. With continued practice and awareness, it becomes easier

to "change the channel" before the emotion attaches and avoid the negativity that comes with it.

- Limit your exposure to violence and negativity. Avoid the news – Most shows focus on what is bad and wrong in the world, thrive on it actually. Such a constant barrage of negativity on society as a whole perpetuates all that is wrong in the world without giving very little attention to what is right. Sure some things you need to be aware of, but the excessive negative focus is of no value to anyone. The news accentuates all that's bad in the world with very little attention being giving to the good things that happen in the world. Good news is boring and doesn't bring ratings but the constant barrage of negativity while ignoring the good is draining and detrimental. As with the law of attraction, what you focus on is given energy. Imagine what a world it would be if the news focused and spread the positives in life.

- On the same tone, avoid violent movies. We live in a society that thrives on movies of fear and torture, the gorier the better it seems. I've never been able to understand why anyone would find enjoyment in such atrocities – Avoid anything that promotes violence including violent video games.

- Simplify life…get rid of all that's not necessary. All the extra activities, stress, drama, all the things designed to please your ego, which is actually a misnomer because the ego will never be pleased or satisfied.

- Try to spend time with like-minded people. When you have a sincere desire to move forward and live through Essence, the universe tends to guide you toward people who have the same thoughts and goals. By the same token, the universe tends to remove those from your life that take you away from your purpose and lower your vibrations through the drama and negativity they present. Sometimes, when it's not possible to remove these people from your life, perhaps maybe a relative, or someone significant you cannot remove, try limiting your exposure to these individuals in order to not be drawn into their drama.,

- Make time to sit in silence every day; whether it be through meditation, or simply sitting in nature in appreciation of all that's around you.

- It is important to practice being aware of your thoughts at all times. Catch your thoughts before the emotion arises. Or if you cannot and the emotion is able to attach itself, don't feed into it with more thoughts. Simply be aware, just watch and observe and the emotion will fade away.

- Slow down – sometimes if you refuse, the universe will find a way for you to slow down for you. For instance, maybe you need to slow down, but refuse to do so. Next thing you know, you find yourself with a broken leg, forcing you to slow down and take a breather. In the long run the cost of a broken leg is far outweighed by the benefit you receive from having the chance to stop, slow down and simplify your life.

- Let go of the need to plan. Part of being in the flow is being open to what comes your way at every given moment. The ego has a desperate need to plan and place life on a nice little schedule. Unfortunately, all this time spent planning rarely works, and often you're so busy planning that you miss the things the flow is bringing your way.

- Practice forgiveness. Forgiveness is not about the other person, but about you. Holding on to anger and negativity impairs your ability to feel gratitude and love.

- Read, read, and read some more. And then read again. Read the books, or websites, or rewatch the videos that influenced you the most. While there does seem to be a point where you have to put down the books and start to experience life, I have found that repetition is the best way to encourage the subconscious mind to come on board. Or if it's a video that's been a major influence, keep it on as background, or fall asleep to it at night. Read or listen to a video before you go to sleep so these thoughts are the last thing your mind focuses on, as opposed to the problems and the dramas of the day. When you wake up in the morning. Start your day reading. If you want to stay in touch with essence while trying to make it in the" real world" it is essential that you reconnect with words on a daily basis, or better still, several times a day

- Even if you are not feeling it, especially when you're not feeling it. Sit down and make a list of the things in your life you are grateful for, don't just think about, actually write it down. When you think, your mind can wander but when you write it requires much more focus from the thinking mind. Although you may not feel it when you start your list, the longer you stay with it, the more gratitude will arise and help put you in touch with Essence.

- Carry something with you throughout the day which you can touch as a reminder to yourself to stop and feel grateful for what you have. It could be a bracelet or necklace, or some kind of memento. Doesn't matter what it is as long as it is a personal reminder to you to be grateful throughout the day.

These practices, while not a cure all, will most definitely help you on your path to living life in Essence. While by no means is this easy, life is a journey, not a destination – always remember that!

Good luck on your journey.
Namaste

ABOUT THE AUTHOR

Robin Masters lives by the Jersey shore with her husband, Bobby. She has two children she adores; a son, Jon, and a daughter, Kaitlin. Robin is an ordained minister of the Universal life Church. She has a passion for writing and hopes this book will touch the lives of many, and hopes it helps those who read it find their way to Essence. Robin may be reached at robinmasters444@gmail.com or at her website, fromegotoessence.org